Commies

by Karen Kellock Ph.D.

Manual for Superior Men

A complete theory based on Einstein physics,
Political Psychology, Systems Theory
and Archetypal Psychiatry.

FORMULA

All success attraction
All disease obstruction
All recovery elimination

You must fast on all three

OBSTRUCTIONS:

People
Habit
Food

COMMIES

The commie spirit is social expectations: share, share, share. Conformity and casual sex expectations, social connections, serial relationships, breakups/broken families. Empaths easily take on neuroses of invaders lest they learn to set boundaries. For this false religion replaces socials for God and humans for divine. Modernity is not into individuation but GROUPS.

COMMIES

AND THE LEVELING SPIRIT:
THE ROUGH ROAD TO GREATNESS

NEVER FIT OR FELT LEGIT
MISFITS HAVE SCHOOL PHOBIA
VISIONS OF FUTURE GRANDEUR
PROPHETS ARE NEVER KNOWN
OUTCASTED AND STIGMATIZED
DESPITE ALL YOUR SMILE IS BRIGHT
YOUR REWARD FOR SURVIVING
ROUGH ROAD TO GREATNESS
SEE THE BLESSING IN DISGUISE
PEOPLE WORSHIP IS A BLOCK
GOD IS OPENING DOORS
WICKED PERSECUTORS
PERIODS OF MENTAL ILLNESS
WAKING UP TO SICK SINS
MEANT TO STAND OUT/SHINE
INSTANT FORGIVENESS
THO' THE INSTIGATORS ARE DEAD
TRANSMUTE HURT TO CREATIVE DRIVE
DIVINE JUSTICE AND COMPENSATION
IT'S HOW THE BRAIN WORKS
LOSING FRIENDS AND FAMILY
YOU'RE ELEVATED HIGH, THEY'RE NOT
DISENTRENCHING FROM OLD NETWORKS
THE EXCELLENT ARE LONELY
LEAVING THE WALKING DEAD

COMMIES

AND THE LEVELING SPIRIT:
THE ROUGH ROAD TO GREATNESS

Most just give in to the communist spirit, the evil drive to bash uniqueness and even to fear it.

The communist spirit is horrible as a leveler. Lopping off heads is the mean outcome and a killer.

Like a boomerang the roles have reversed. As the top becomes the bottom you now come first.

They stink, having accomplished nothing in life. They were the most popular, remember? Aye

You weren't meant to fit in, you were meant to stand out. But a stigma can make you feel nuts.

You were the lame one, the weird one. But it was a blessing in disguise in the end, a ton.

Your siblings called you crazy, a narcissist with delusions of grandeur, even a criminal see.

NEVER FIT OR FELT LEGIT

You could never fit or feel legit. They ruined your self esteem and taunted you to have crying fits.

This drove you down to bad habits to cope. Anything that lightened your load like food/dope.

Your young life became clouded this way and you searched for your self in future decades.

You were odd, they reacted & you took it bad. Not knowing your destiny you couldn't fight back.

COMMIES and the LEVELING SPIRIT

You were meant for big things and they were small groupthinks. The early life of greats stinks.

I was so scared of my peers I hated school, parties, sunday school or church camp outings.

MISFITS HAVE SCHOOL PHOBIA

I developed school phobia which lasted 'til graduate school: I preferred being alone/away from ya'.

At sixth grade camp I spent time in the infirmary missing mommy who I wrote constantly.

My first beer at fifteen took a ton off my shoulders. It was like enlightenment making me bolder.

Some of the greatest died of alcoholism. For me addiction was the great obstacle overcome.

When sisters came back from liberal colleges they turned on the heat: they were so mean.

VISIONS OF FUTURE GRANDEUR

I dreamed of future days when things wouldn't be this way. They called that grandiose and mental ok.

I can recall these feelings now and they were horrible. All in the gut, the solar plexus detects it all.

Even now I hate get-togethers. I feel so out of place and cannot relate. Simply put, I feel their hate.

Meant to stand out, this predicament led to a STIGMA which they constantly gossiped about.

If only I could've seen ahead to future fame instead. But I relied on pot, beer and wanting to be dead.

COMMIES and the LEVELING SPIRIT

Once they pegged me as bad I had a stigma to deal with and got like an abusive drunk: very mad.

How'd I know what was going on? It took years of study to see the matrix of stigma vs. future renown.

No counselor told me: "the reason you're down is cuz you're a misfit priming for future renown".

PROPHETS ARE NEVER KNOWN

Prophets are never known in their own town or family. They basically will hate him usually.

They are outcasted, ridiculed, derided and stigmatized with nasty lies til they just wanted to die.

Outcasted in your home town, the blessing was you shifted to be on top while they stayed down.

It's called enontiodromia: everything shifted to it's opposite while the top became the bottom.

Bottom to the top, top to the bottom: the joyous outcome of a shitty childhood seen as clown.

OUTCASTED AND STIGMATIZED

Being outcasted and stigmatized you figured you had something wrong with you, so despised.

But God saw you in the end--who you would be--and unbeknownst to you took em all out early.

YOU were the one God wanted to use for a time like this, when boring sameness is seen as bliss.

They were the set up for commie takeover, when anything that doesn't fit is shamed forever.

COMMIES and the LEVELING SPIRIT

You were the one to be BRIGHT, shining on darkness that heretofore created your madness.

They thought they were better than you so as you rise up it's a slap in the face to the whole crew.

"Delusions of grandeur, who do you think you are, you're not a star!": only overcome by getting sober.

Satan ridiculed, made fun of and outcasted you so you wouldn't see your worth and destiny too.

It's all a setup for the communist spirit of low threshold limits for differences and novelty flare ups.

After resolving all that you shine bright like the sun. You've matured tho' the past was no fun.

DESPITE ALL YOUR SMILE IS BRIGHT

Despite all that your smile is bright and you've a beautiful soul which is out of sight.

You survived what most couldn't stand: to be rejected as weird or odd and to have no friends.

They were blind, slow and dumb and thus rejected you, the most intelligent and kindly one.

It is hell looking back but take a look to see how far you've come and what you've overcome.

The road to greatness was rough and filled with hatefulness. Be grateful your highness.

Your intelligence is transcendent and global, the peasants didn't see it or saw it as awful.

YOUR REWARD FOR SURVIVING

COMMIES and the LEVELING SPIRIT

As your reward for surviving and thriving God pays you back double or in most cases, tenfold.

Had there not been so much to overcome you wouldn't have matured as one of the great ones.

It wasn't meant for them to see the real you. They were your challenge for betterment, your trial too.

And when you fully matured, they fell away. God turned his wrath on them on that archetypal day.

Whether it was sister abuse, neighbor jealousy or a childhood bully, you built social muscle see.

You females had to learn about mean men and how to build a wall between you and fake friends.

You men had to learn about flighty unstable women in this age and how to discern the good ok.

ROUGH ROAD TO GREATNESS

You were stubborn so to make you learn you had to overcome rogues/foes with nowhere to turn.

To learn about narcissists so were wiped out financially or emotionally until you saw God exists.

All these events provided fire to make gold. It burned the dross so now you're bright and bold.

I'm sorry you went thru this, my God it was torture but look what it produced: a brand new nature.

God hid your value--the diamond that you are--so you could flourish alone until matured as a star.

SEE THE BLESSING IN DISGUISE

COMMIES and the LEVELING SPIRIT

See the blessing in disguise. These people are shocked you made it so it's a lesson for them too guys.

You're a natural beauty and don't need anyone. But God spread your buffet in front of em, what fun.

Your detractors gotta stay on the farm cuz they never did anything to get past it, just strong-arm.

You were hurt so much you can write of it forever, helping the masses so now they can recover.

Don't ever expect to get them back, that old scaffold for your growth is now thrown in the trash.

You not fitting in was a blessing in disguise as you shot forward in reaction while their soul dies.

People are cruel but only greats know this. The others are deluded thinking they're "good" sis.

PEOPLE WORSHIP IS A BLOCK

People-worship is a major block to God. You don't have this now, you know what people are not.

Don't look back but focus on your future. When memory triggers pain say "NO!" and mature.

They're watching you, admiring or even hating you. That's how systems revert when on top Sue.

Whether they're inspired or jealous, you're so high in a new place it doesn't matter your highness.

They're stuck in the past but you're having a blast as God opens doors so profitable and vast!

You held your tongue when you wanted to kill em. This built social muscle so you made millions.

COMMIES and the LEVELING SPIRIT

GOD IS OPENING DOORS

God is opening doors that your enemies could never conceive. It's double for your trouble see.

Now continue to shine and be happy you were an outcast for when that reverses it's a blast!

Forget your miserable hometown you were never meant to fit. It's the path to greatness but now you're it.

They thought you weren't good enough for them back then so they're not good enough for you friend.

WICKED PERSECUTORS

Wicked persecutors have dirty minds they projected onto you with false accusations, aye.

Small minds love to talk about the one who won't adapt and they say horrible things [just crap].

The "decent" old ladies are the worst. They get wind of something and take off, cursing you first.

The more ridiculous the more they'll believe it but calumny will be judged and you'll see it.

When misjudged & accused it's hard not taking it on, but recall it's all on them, the wicked throng.

They see themselves in the right and you in the wrong just for being you, but just wait/sit tight.

They can't abide your vivid differences and small minds always think like this but God will dis.

The more weak the more they misspeak about you, God's kid who He strengthens to be unique.

COMMIES and the LEVELING SPIRIT

Gossip is what keeps their system going and tho' it's hard to take it's how the herd keeps moving.

Don't think about these things any more: close that old door cuz it's how Satan keeps you floored.

The more weak the more they misspeak about you, God's kid who He made so great and unique.

PERIODS OF MENTAL ILLNESS

You may have had periods of mental illness due to all this but it's instantly solved with repentance.

The felt rejection was so bad you sunk into promiscuity to feel closeness: just more repentance.

It's a wake up call: your sinful reactions to it all, ways to find solace after any mistreatment at all.

Addictions used to cope: alcohol, food, sex or dope when you reached the end of your rope.

The sin was a coping mechanism til it became too high a price to high for a payoff dwindling each day.

Your oddness was your creativity unrecognized then sin was a response to being utterly despised.

WAKING UP TO SICK SINS

One wakes up midlife to realize they were a slut cuz sex was utlized to fit in, to not hurt, to not die.

God your Father just wants your love, to admit it and to repent--that's ALL. Just return to the ball.

An unrepentant sinner is stuck in delusion until one day he wakes up to his entire sick situation.

COMMIES and the LEVELING SPIRIT

I cried all night in God's arms and He simply said "it's over, just forget it--return to your charms."

I drank, ate, smoked and snorted as a substitute for mother love. Tho' deluded, it was rough.

That was my response to their response to my oddness. With repentance it became creative boldness.

I have no bad habits today and demons have gone away. I watch what I eat or a high price to pay.

Just be nice, you know how to. Do your work and be honest, you've got to. That's all, just cruise.

Dress nice, you've got style. You know it all so don't worry over mental illness just run that mile.

It's not faking it, it's just acting right [as taught] until you make it. Be civilized and actually love it.

You were sick just as many are sick. But you were intelligent so you got right and quick.

MEANT TO STAND OUT/SHINE

You were always meant to stand out and shine beyond the foolishness, a reaction to the swine.

I realized one day I'd been mentally ill thru an entire marriage. Things said or done were an outrage.

Delusions fueled by vicious games working subconsciously to trigger demons ok.

Mental illness is triggered interjectionally. In relationship we find ourselves in trouble mentally.

You thought your spouse was the problem til one day you see it all: you were the raging automaton.

COMMIES and the LEVELING SPIRIT

You didn't leave the rejecting childhood unscathed. It all came out in these various ways.

INSTANT FORGIVENESS

How glorious: After all this, it's over in a minute. Just take it to the cross and your Father forgives it.

If mom was a raging drunk you think: I'll never be like that nut but guess what: it all came out.

God knows all these complexities of why we became sinners and forgives it all, now we're winners.

Don't worry about the haters, justified or not. It all disappears and then you're back on top.

You weren't good enough for them back in the day but now they're not on your level today.

Like a boomerang the roles have reversed and they're not good enough for you anymore dearest.

Those voted most likely to succeed turned out to have fleas so get offa your knees/do your expertise.

THO' THE INSTIGATORS ARE DEAD

These blocks are still in your brain & tho' the instigators are dead they're still in your head.

Let em continue to hate/envy, you're outshining the dark energy they're in see. Now just be happy.

The one they rejected, ridiculed and treated like a dog in the street turned out to be so smart & sweet.

They put these insecurities on you and it lasted and to deal with the black cloud you got addicted.

COMMIES and the LEVELING SPIRIT

Like a persecuted Indian in a TV western, your drunks were the worst from the awful frustration.

They blamed me for everything. I was scapegoated for years and I drank to confirm their disparaging.

I wore the black cloud like a robe and they were suspicious of everything I said, did or wrote.

Doing this to an odd child is a crime but this Ph.D. in the Streets produced the bold style of mine.

TRANSMUTE HURT TO CREATIVE DRIVE

So pissed off I dare not drink, I transmuted the whole thing to a creative drive to express it see.

Their "popularity" was all they could see plus you not fitting so obviously just made em crazy.

This is called Social Hypnotism and it's the basis of all communism. It's the spirit of doom son.

If you don't fit you're not legit and it's a matter of degree where it leads: to prison/death/drunken fits.

To this degree their twisted brains are filled with booze, drugs and the foolish thoughts they bought.

Their high school mentality won't allow em to see you for the person you are, a potential star.

Your narcissistic mom couldn't see it either and it was particularly bad with your abusive sisters.

Communism isn't just about government, it starts with the social hypnotism in the peasants.

Their mealy brains produce radical change. Drop a thought and they'll put landlords in chains.

COMMIES and the LEVELING SPIRIT

Even after getting well I'll regress into this doomsday hell of ME being the problem, like a spell.

The anti-communist spirit is independence, uniqueness and wholeness as God designed for all of us.

Though you did nothing to these people, that's just how they feel about you. It is an evil mind-screw.

So that's what happened to you, the weird one. Childhood was no fun but you excelled hon'.

They can't focus on anything but you while you never think of them having higher things to pursue.

DIVINE JUSTICE AND COMPENSATION

You compensated with work while they never accomplished a thing putting them first.

The outcast either dies in the gutter or becomes best of the litter, a bright star getting even better.

The one voted the LEAST likely to succeed became the most successful creating things we need.

The one everyone thought was crazy became the most successful, a pretty diamond shining brightly.

There is always a divine justice to life. Everything evens out in the end, making all wrongs right.

Enantiodromia--where the top becomes the bottom & the bottom becomes the top: how we love ya'.

The best revenge is truly success. Of you just getting better after being humiliated/seen as less.

It will happen: keep your eyes on the goal. No matter what they do, be like Trump and persevere y'all.

COMMIES and the LEVELING SPIRIT

Hah: The more dirt they threw on your name the more you became a celebrity of growing fame.

You fought the commie spirit and won. This was like climbing the highest mountain, good job hon'

Public humiliation and disgrace was your greatest teacher to remain dignified in every case.

You look like a celebrity in front of your naysayers who made you an outcast. That success will last.

Your hometown won't see the diamond in the rough nor allow you to get up and show your stuff.

There's a leveling process in the herd which I call the Communist Spirit. This is it, don't fear it.

IT'S HOW THE BRAIN WORKS

It's the way the brain works but the ego too. It's how small minds think so give up your old crew.

Small minds populate the communist spirit while big minds are cut off and abandoned from it.

It's the intelligentsia, forerunners and pathbreakers who are killed first. Anyone first is seen as cursed.

Elites don't go to their high school reunions while the others love and flock to those situations.

Now you continue to flourish and shine and leave these miserable godforsaken people behind.

They are not fit to go with you to the next level, on your journey to success while being God blessed.

Anticipation! Stop looking at your email cuz the past is gone and the future hasn't arrived yet hon'.

COMMIES and the LEVELING SPIRIT

In peacetime we're treated well but in wartime it's like a hell. In both cases a strong man feels swell.

LOSING FRIENDS AND FAMILY

The more you grow the more you lose family and friends. Even as I say it this seems ridiculous.

You're just nothing like these people anymore. It's a part of this life and needs to be accepted bro'.

As you grow as a person you drift further and further away. Don't let this be a stumbling block ok?

Millions stay with old friends and family their entire lives. But you felt there was more, aye.

You were never born to fit in but to stand out, to do great things and that meant being left out.

If you're chosen you're an outcast. Accept it, glory in it and don't feel bad about it, you're the best.

Suddenly you're excluded and even disinvited. You may feel wretched, repugnant or even hated.

YOU'RE ELEVATED HIGH, THEY'RE NOT

You're elevated very high, you're specialized, you can only relate to maximum/equal level guys.

It's just the way the cookie crumbles or the herd splits and there is little you can do about it.

They don't seem to take life seriously or face the facts. They likely even resent how you do that.

You try hard in life and they do not. That's when they shame you for it and it can get very rough.

COMMIES and the LEVELING SPIRIT

Outcasts are hated cuz they started like the others but then changed the most--at a high cost.

You outgrew things and they did not. Who do you think you are to transcend the pack you nut?

It's a major shakeup in life. Just when you got going there's all this strife but keep persevering, aye.

They start to drive you crazy but then you think: why am I even attached to them this easily?

DISENTRENCHING FROM OLD NETWORKS

Disentrenching from old networks is a major step in life and few talk about it cuz it's so sad, aye.

You turn focus on yourself: why am I trying to get their validation, having nothing more in common?

Why am I trying to get them to understand what I'm doing? Why is this important in pursuing?

They're out partying at night while you're studying and getting up the next morning feeling right.

You're making decisions affecting the rest of your life while they are self-indulging day and night.

What you do in this 24 hours dictates your future and they don't understand that for sure.

You gotta leave these people behind bro', that's what you gotta do. It's sad I know but be through.

They're backstabbers and backbiters, they're jealous of you sis. It's hard to imagine it's come to this.

Some actors stayed with childhood friends but it's very rare and usually involved supporting them.

COMMIES and the LEVELING SPIRIT

Haters will say anything to discredit you: The most embarrassing and nasty things too.

Things sisters said about me gave me sleepless nights wrenching in sweats over their filthy lies.

They didn't just hurt me it was devastating that anyone would even think such things see.

At the rate your going it's no wonder you continue to lose friends, family and others brother.

Loneliness is part of the greatness trip. it's hard to get over it but look to new horizons/get a grip.

THE EXCELLENT ARE LONELY

The excellent are lonely in the communist spirit. That's the intention, to make us controlled by it.

We weren't born to be around those we were born around. We're meant to grow not drown.

They don't understand you and never will. They don't want to see you grow & expand even still.

You'll always have birth connections, of course. But you'll never be close, don't count on it bro'.

Getting close to new people you'll put loyalty first. You never felt that from siblings, feeling cursed.

Family togetherness is a myth, a dangerous one. Listen to misgivings in your gut, they're profound.

We simply grew up around people not meant for us. We're meant for much better, it's a promise.

They were low vibrational people knowing what to say & when to smile but never run that extra mile.

COMMIES and the LEVELING SPIRIT

Go to family dinners and feel you're the only one alive. it's unreal, surrealistic and sickening, aye.

You give them things and they reward you with rocks. They're nothing and I pray you find that out.

It sux being around those people and you hate get togethers. You'd rather be alone forever.

Wanna have a deep conversation? Nope, too scary for them. Wanna take a swim? No, they can't.

You're too much for them and thus you feel so alone. Life's too short man, get going/be gone.

LEAVING THE WALKING DEAD

They're not even living, they're the walking dead. Don't even give em a minute, walk tall instead.

You don't exist in their matrix, no--you're an outcast. Don't even try to make it, walk tall at last.

Elevate in life & find better people in this world. There are many to appreciate such a great boy/girl.

If you're not driven, ask yourself why this is. Was it something those nobodies said sis?

Keep that inner drive alive. If you don't you will die. Walking zombies surround us daily, aye.

They're all haters and they don't love you. That's the absolute truth about the human zoo.

There's no love to be had and no love to be found. Move on, that's my advice and I've been around.

I saw the truth as a teen and was forced to be around them anyway. It was torture in those days.

COMMIES and the LEVELING SPIRIT

Their hearts are beating but they're not alive. You're full of life, a star and creative genius, no jive.

They're boring/not any fun. You hate being with em yet the fantasy keeps livin' and you've gotta run.

People are dumbed down, lazy and selfish. Escape the scene & find people you admire and relish.

Stay away from sluggish gainsayers and find ambitious pathbreakers. What a difference to seekers!

To those I've known from my childhood town: you're sluggish & boring as hell and I'm moving on.

These are some big truths and not everyone can accept and make it through. Stay put then, adieu.

Commies
Preface

COMMIE SPIRIT & SOCIAL EXPECTATIONS
HERO'S JOURNEY VS. COMMIES
HEART BREAKS FOR SOUL TO HEAL
PRECIOUS LESSONS IN A CABIN
HYPERSENSITIVE INTROVERTS
SOUL TIES
RECOVERY AFTER BEING GAMED
QUEENS AND CLOWNS: OUCH!

Commies

Commies

Commies

COMMIE SPIRIT & SOCIAL EXPECTATIONS

It was the communist social spirit which prevailed. Communitas, commune, I despised it all.

They were commies from kindergarten: share, share. This was the post WWII spirit I declare.

Then it's all about casual sex. Casual sex and the communist spirit--amoral, illicit--is expected.

Group and sex expectations, social connections, serial relationships, breakups, broken families.

Not independent study, hobbies, projects, growth decisions and individuation but GROUPS.

The false church acted like my dislike of socials meant I disliked God. Social is God, human is divine.

I loved God but hated those church retreats. I was homesick & freaked out by the other kids.

HERO'S JOURNEY VS. COMMIES

Don't get mad just realize they're stupid. That's why they put ridiculous projections on you kid.

Some battles can only be won by outliving the enemy. Wait, prepare, sorry it has to be this way.

Gossip is how they rule their domain and jealousy is in their DNA. That's how women are, sad to say.

COMMIES

When you think of backstabbing think of Christ who suffered the ultimate when it comes to bullying.

See you were born different from them and then in your protective isolation went way beyond em hon'

Retirement is bliss cuz you're falling outa these structures. Like slipping on cozy pajamas.

Gossip all you want I'm behind my locked gate and it's none of my business what you think.

You can't control me anymore if I've forgiven myself. That was the last block before success.

I came from a sheltered home and knew nothing about people but learned fast leaving the castle.

It was commie Southern California and young boys ruled small towns and the cops did nothing.

HEART BREAKS FOR SOUL TO HEAL

Let your heart break and your soul will heal. Realize you were gamed/manipulated like a naive girl.

The only way to break out of this bondage is to accept the pain. The shell cracks then you're free.

You've been in denial so when you wake up it's the exact same thing: pain, then you're free.

You lived in a fantasy Sue, assuming relationships work out beautifully just cuz you want em to.

You must view things as they are, not your fantasy about em or how they could be better.

He invites you to stay on his beautiful Arabian horse ranch then you're his prisoner, horrors.

COMMIES

I escaped beautiful Arabian horse ranch for a tiny dusty cabin in the wilderness: independence.

That was part of my Ph.D. in the streets. Something. a normal person raised right would never need.

When making life decisions like where you're living, see the facts and keep your fantasies empty.

In my tiny dusty cabin built year of my birth [waiting for me empty] I was joyful with mirth, blissfully.

After having to adapt to that old creep [something I can't now believe] I value freedom differently.

A man can look SO good and you start to fantasize but live with him and enter a den disguised.

In a flash I realized what he was and I was trapped. His friends were there, hell is where I was at.

PRECIOUS LESSONS IN A CABIN

God gave me a precious lesson about privacy and freedom in a short time then He freed me.

It's the same thing about people coming over. When they're here I gotta adapt-
-no more.

Still I lacked a fence in the wilderness so the rare times frenemies came I felt I was going insane.

I still feel like a cat in a room full of rocking chairs just thinking about it, see I'm a super-sensitive.

Worse than people imposing on me was being gamed or degraded by soul ties but I have survived.

Hypersensitive empaths/introverts must get tough setting boundaries or they're invaded constantly.

COMMIES

HYPERSENSITIVE INTROVERTS

Hypersensitive introverts easily take on neuroses of invaders lest they learn to set boundaries.

I suffered in the dessert but developed ways to recover from the game while destiny's reclaimed.

Setting boundaries pisses the narcissist off: I coulda been killed way out there with no cops.

That Jezebel invaded me with her army of flying monkeys, so jealous was she of my privacy.

I can't believe it happened, it's like a dream. But here I sit behind a gate and life is fascinating.

My helpful friend Dr. Paris told me I had a rare disease: people make me sick, like a dam lunatic.

God gave me a mate who understands me when no one does. Always one good friend the bible says.

Fairweather friends are everywhere. They come and go, they lovebomb then ghost, true is rare.

SOUL TIES

I finally realized it was a dam soul tie--not love, desire for marriage, soul mate or love of my life!

How are soul ties established? Thru sex which is as common as going to the bathroom, a hex.

To y'all: These lessons were painful and I apologize to anyone who had to witness it in this gal.

Part of Hero's journey is dark night of the soul, a deep cavern of demons you're confronting of old.

COMMIES

I felt degraded by their expectations of conformity like they were superior, felt it from a young girl.

But then with sin comes shame and then you're controlled by others, losing independence.

RECOVERY AFTER BEING GAMED

If you embrace the pain of withdrawal it's pregnant with possibilities, what you receive is incredible.

I called it PTSD: I couldn't get over being gamed, I had intrusive thoughts and controlled by shame.

You may crave the synthetic love you had for so long despite empty esteem/diminishing a queen

Synthetic love was never real it just separated you from yourself. It was a dream but reality was hell.

A craving for plastic love is the main symptom of withdrawal–it's all you've ever known after all.

The devil calls you back: there'll never be anyone but Jack. Withdrawal clears this out fairly quick.

Tho' this man is shallow and depleted of character you're not thinking of that, you want inferior.

QUEENS AND CLOWNS: OUCH!

Tho' he's inferior intellectually and spiritually you shamelessly let him get a grip on you honey.

But it really wasn't him but the fake dream the system set you up to pursue: all fantasy it seems.

That system conditions you to fall prey to someone like this: it's a collusion to hold you down sis.

COMMIES

There are jewels in your pain & shame called lessons. We must bear em but they won't happen again.

Scorners delight in their scorning and fools hate knowledge but wisdom's always crying out.

The megaphone of wisdom is a painful experience teaching you more than a library of books.

Commies

SOCIAL TYRANNY STARTS EARLY

When I entered Kindergarten I felt it immediately: social tyranny, the set up for communism likely.

The loss of individual liberties, the right to be, was stripped from us in a drought/mental tyranny.

Communists are into conformity and tyranny and that is the basis of sibling abuse and treachery.

It was no big thing but your sister made it a BIG thing until you lost your mind in her tyranny.

It's almost like part of the selfhood path is public opprobrium of the pitiful hero fallen.

I felt I was in a vice the minute I entered the place. It's a cruel tyranny the social, now pugnacious.

I felt communist spirit when I entered the place, tho' I called it something different it was hellish.

SOCIAL IMPOSITIONS

Borrego taught me the value of privacy cuz when people came it would drive me crazy suddenly.

Setting boundaries is such a slap in their face they'll create smear campaigns to retaliate.

You're supposed to open your doors to them and all their friends, no vetting just social skills.

COMMIES

This social thing is setting us up for communism--of being in a big pen altogether, globalism.

The victims of the narcissist experience characteristic shame, humiliation and embarrassment.

Trauma: a reaction to shock. Complex PTSD: the reaction to repeated/prolonged shocks.

Many victims of narcissistic abuse behave recklessly without knowing why. It's a "help" cry.

SIBLING ABUSE A SILENT EPIDEMIC

Sibling abuse is a silent epidemic. Heck abuse victims are attacked even if they mention it.

Sibling abuse and bullying is a hidden epidemic. Ignored as rivalry it causes trauma and getting sick.

Sibling abuse is most common but least reported, higher than child or spouse abuse combined.

The consequences into adulthood are similar to parent-child abuse but due to secrecy even worse.

Tho' 80% of siblings experience maltreatment it's called the forgotten abuse cuz no one believes it.

There are 40 million sibling abuse survivors in America alone, let that sink in about the home.

Sibling rivalry is fighting, tattling, frustrations, demanding and competing for attention.

What starts as rivalry can escalate into full scale abuse in teen years and throughout adulthood.

The core of sibling abuse is intent to harm and control in repeated patterns lasting months or decades.

COMMIES

One sibling takes the role of aggressor while the other sibling feels regularly disempowered.

Usually the older will dominate the younger, pushing em around, gaslighting in order to disempower.

Toxic siblings will destroy your career, reputation and everything about you. It's rough and cruel.

SIBLING ABUSE STRIKES TERROR

Unlike rivalry the purpose of sibling abuse is to establish superiority and strike terror for control see.

Factors: the motives, degree of severity, the power of imbalance and effects of prolonged trauma.

Signs: one is aggressive, the other feels helpless and powerless--a definite imbalance of power.

Many siblings are jealous of each other and it gets to a point of extreme destruction for sure.

The bully sibling could be terrorizing the other with pathological lying, degradation, whatever.

Retaliation. Once the one sibling sets healthy boundaries the other is furious with envy.

Of course sibling abuse is a worldwide silent epidemic: those with whom we have regular contact.

They lie, steal and cheat. They will try to steal the sibling's possessions including her husband.

SPREADING RUMORS

If they don't physically abuse their sibling they spread rumors seeking to ruin her reputation.

COMMIES

By far the biggest sibling abuse is emotional. This is psychological abuse, traumatic as hell.

Some will have their friends gang up on their sibling or scapegoated relative, man it is criminal.

Unstable siblings sadistically like enjoying watching their sibling suffer. Keep your pets closer.

Many people are sociopathic or narcissistic--very mentally unstable and unpredictable.

ENJOYMENT OF SUFFERING

He enjoys watching his sibling suffer: sociopathic, psychopathic, narcissist or whatever.

Just by one setting boundaries the other will triangulate [collude] with the others to block/destroy.

Every culture varies on degrees of acceptability. "He beat me cuz he loves me from jealousy."

They hire attorneys against the sibling, they blame-shift and get the flying monkeys against him.

This system is so predictable and yet sibling abuse is rarely discussed though it's a hell hole.

They withhold important information from the sibling, like legal docs or he got half the house.

They may steal the trust fund or inheritance because, again, they want to punish the sibling.

They need to punish the sibling to such an extent they will steal what is their legal birthright.

If you're experiencing repeated trauma from sibling abuse you'll have complex PTSD too.

COMMIES

ADULT SURVIVORS OF SIBLING ABUSE

PTSD, anxiety, depression, emptiness, nightmares, SHAME, embarrassment, suicidation.

Disassociation, triggers, flashbacks, hypervigilance or the fight/flight/freeze/fawn response.

This is not about what's wrong with you, sibling. It's what happened to you due to jealousy.

Eating disorders, addictions, panic attacks, phobias, insomnia and autoimmune conditions.

MUST IDENTIFY YOUR TORMENTORS

The stages of survivor recovery require him to identify what took place. Sorry Jane and Grace.

Name what happened: sibling abuse. Name the abusers, now memories come into view.

Let go of the toxic shame. Understand this is the major game and you've been the recipient ok.

The shame is from you vs. the whole pack. You're an outsider now but it's good you woke up.

90% of abusive siblings deny they ever abused their sibling and will not take accountability.

We can't change or force them to speak the truth about the abuse, but we can get support, whew.

A scapegoat may not see he's been discarded. It may last for years, an eerie sense trust is rotted.

At one point the fog--denial--lifts and we see the light. Fragments come together = insight.

COMMIES

It hurts to suddenly be in the dark having been discarded and with everyone disinvited.

OUR OWN UNIQUE TALENTS

You have a peculiarly unique talent and should just be doing that. It's so obvious but few do it.

You love me, you hold me together and wall off those creeps the non-birds of a feather.

They tried to whip my spirit outa me, to make me conform. I just went mad/couldn't believe it.

I always wanted to do my own thing/go my own way and have my own opinions but that brought hatred.

All I want is privacy, provision and protection to do my work and that takes a partner or it's all worse.

It's great you have followers but are you misleading them? That's the thing God abhors so have caution.

I made it thus far all because I didn't do things to make money but to find my self but who am I to say.

HAUNTED HOUSE OF SPIRITS

Can't you see he's a thousand people in one? He multi-adapts to all scenes but has no inner home.

Extreme arrogance/sense of entitlement--that was high school '85 so what are they like now man.

They have poor coping skills: if you disagree you're the enemy, dead--and that's why you agree.

All that interests me is you can do manly things. Home fascinates and brings my respect darling.

COMMIES

Taking selfies has always been important especially in times of dehumanization, to present SELF.

The dehumanized concentration camp prisoner takes a selfie to maintain his identity and dignity.

You can disable the neuropathways through time, work and separation from the false/gross buddy.

A grasshopper in their eyes, I didn't feel like I existed. That I call: depersonalization of the Elected.

The Elect are kicked out. There's something about em that they hate and want banned from the earth.

Liberal women don't raise their sons right. They raise em to be angry girls not patriotic, loyal and polite.

Disable the neuropathways of your attraction to false buddies: separate, time/work, relocate.

BROKEN RED FLAG DETECTOR

Abuse in childhood is what wrecks our red flag detector so we're actually attracted to dangerous fakers.

There's a tremendous cost to no filter about who gets into your life. It's decline/death or YOU decide.

You end up with people not connected to you or who are incapable of understanding the depth of a muse.

When your red flag detector is broken your life is riddled with broken people using/fooling you, forsaken.

These drip dry hangers will leave you more broken from before you knew them, that's certain hon'.

BOUNDARIES ARE EVERYTHING

COMMIES

The more bad gets in the more boundaries fall apart and then **EVEN WORSE** get in, I've experienced it.

Every time someone else came in more life was sucked out of me until the body fell apart too see.

To heal you must quickly recognize those who are not good for you but victims don't have a clue.

Red flags are signs the sick give off--that they're not safe/what they seem or emotionally unavailable.

Face what people are [philistine rabble] then protect yourself and it's all ok-- the problem is naiveté.

What's ok/what's not ok: in abusive childhoods we shut down our natural instincts to adapt every day.

One loses the "good" vulnerability--being allowed to feel things, detect threats, call out their intentions.

It was good we went numb back then--to blunt exposure to evil--but numb now means can't see people.

If still stuck in old battles with the rabble you still haven't accepted most humans are going to hell.

Unhealthy intruders will pressure you to override your natural fears. Don't do it and just persevere.

You feel it's wrong or dangerous and they push you by calling you a "prude" or "chicken"--ignore this.

If you don't have good boundaries/grow up denying your reality it's easy to go against your ears/eyes.

With early trauma you second guess yourself: am I mistaken here? NO, and this is dangerous.

None of it applies anymore, the perpetrators are gone or dead but the ghosts drive me mad instead.

COMMIES

With Complex PTSD the need for people is so deep and unmet you'll hang out with rabble, no threat.

TOO CHUMMY TOO FAST

You meet someone, you don't treat em like your new best friend or soul mate. You take it REAL EASY.

Complex PTSD is also known as Crappy Childhood or ACES: Adverse Childhood Experiences.

New research shows early trauma and strife is so related to a multitude of terrible outcomes in life.

Growing up like that is like a culture, mindset or tribe--along with attractions to the same types.

Solution: brain training, soul searching, earning rules of acting like a mature/responsible human being.

Part of excellent action and success is patience. Instead of swearing at delay just say "not a good day."

You take care of the manly stuff, I do my female thing and it's as simple as that--two houses are best.

HOME LIFE AND SOLITUDE

Found a safe place, got it together and relocated. But a woman can't be alone, that's a fact/don't want it.

No one wants solitude more than I do so you can rest assured I will never bother you.

But you'll be close by in case something happens: I just wanna make it thru this life with gladness.

So you found yourself in a beautiful house with the love of your life: That's how our God does things, aye?

COMMIES

Brain training: when the memory intrudes, sub with what you're presently doing to dim neuropathways.

Soul searching: Just be alone, an accomplishment. Look at the soaring suicides cuz most can't stand it.

With PTSD when around people it's complete confusion or boredom and solitude's my only solution.

What most people call "social" is to me complete bedlam and I just wanna scream, in the churches even.

THE FALLEN SOCIAL CHURCHES

We have become a most inferior culture: fat, immoral, ugly, zombies, spiritual blanks, disheveled.

Against the backdrop of mediocrity/emptiness the champions stand out, rest assured honey.

Women run churches. They came to me and DEMANDED I attend their boring socials, key to salvation.

Who get's the deacon's roles? Those who are most SOCIAL. Mrs. Social Charm's now an elder.

You think they'll make a introverted anti-social recluse a deacon in the church? No, they're a curse.

Mr. Social Charm succeeds in church hierarchy, academia, big corps and even medicine: hmmm.

I hated the church socials with a passion and I let it be known! No chatting in the sanctuary crones.

I would say "what do socials have to do with salvation?" and the women would bash me right down.

My country neighborhood of 40 1-acre households are so happy in their homes they don't want socials.

COMMIES

The current resident won't lift a finger, there's no joint effort. If you're interested, what a great respite!

They acted like I was IMMORAL or very SINFUL cuz I hated their socials. Think of the implications.

COMMIE CHRISTIANITY IS SOCIAL

Christianity is about forgiveness of sins, folks--not all this! So we can be clean again cuz HE atoned.

I hate the fact decades in church were lost cuz I gave up in frustration. Holy Rollers come again.

And the female preachers stomping across the floor HAMMERING in their point or course.

What.can be done? Nothing--the churches have fallen and everyone's profitin' with false doctrine.

Don't wanna hear hollering females preaching cuz I"m a hollering female and mom was too tho' a lady.

I wanna believe it's all about God giving me what I want like success as Joel promises but...it's not.

The problem is SIN blocks success--it's a dirty mess affecting all of us--but Jesus solved it sis.

I don't wanna preach cuz I'd be yelling. For the sake of remaining a humble servant I'll stick to writing.

We're just gonna have to wait until it manifests. At least we have the divine plan down, it's the best.

Please don't slip back anymore. You don't look good wearing lower archetypes/become a bore.

If you wanna fly with me I do things the best way and I believe in discussing it in household parlés.

COMMIES

GRATUITOUS SEX EVERYWHERE

You get 3/4 through a fabulous movie and then a gratuitous sex scene is thrown in, so embarrasin'

I even saw a gratuitous. sex scene on the History Channel as Billy the Kid mated her on a saloon table.

Enough of the gratuitous sex scenes! Just to get approval of a debauched society ya think?

It's all about smiling, cheesecake, selfies with friends, creating an image: don't do any of this.

The question is: can you handle it? Can you hitch your boat to it feeling enriched not belittled?

I even read a gratuitous sex scene in a book on astronomy! They gotta inject it in, oh my.

Christian mystics are always alone. But if you could have a marriage of two there's no comparison.

The immigrant flood will continue year after year until it is stopped.

Kindness to strangers is cruelty to your own children. Europe will wake up or die, brethren.

Majority of whites are good people but we've been fed this lie that they are hateful and evil.

"Western Chauvinism" is: an exuberant love and appreciation for everything the west is.

A nation is people, people are a nation. When you bring in strange cultures all the greatness is gone.

Calling us xenophobic cuz we want just our own is an insult.

WE DON'T OWE OUR COUNTRY TO THE WHOLE WORLD

COMMIES

We don't owe our country to the rest of the world.

Those who despise themselves will be despised by others. Alex Gualand

They simply assert it: "Diversity is our strength", end of argument.

The democrats love immigration due to false compassion and the desire to win elections.

If they're globalists in the way they govern they're making a mint and their income is doublin'

But sorry, nationalism is now contagious and mainstream.

White Christian men are the most hated species on earth. Never cower, stand against the curse.

Former FLOTUS Michelle Obama: The root of all problems is "the white man". Go away crazy woman.

Marxists want open borders--they despise Christian culture and know barbarians would crush her.

We don't want em here!

They care nothing for border children just their own power and will use any argument to get there.

The stakes could not be higher, we're talking about America.

The biggest, stupidest and most dangerous 21st century myth: "Diversity is our greatest strength".

Just as the whites have most diversity they are also hated more than anytime in their history.

Conservatives are the only relief from the prevailing mind-numbing orthodoxy of racial diversity.

Diversity is a failed social experiment imposed upon innocent peoples which is possibly insoluble.

COMMIES

To them It's got to be done, our destiny: to feed on each other's differences and make history.

CENSORSHIP AND WITCH HUNTS

They're gonna make it work, forcing the fit. They won't stop until we're all dead thru a failed myth.

The media acts as though the demographic drivers of this crisis are nonexistent: RIP CNN.

The problem is immorality, family breakdown and mass immigration from antithetical societies not racism.

Conflict is between white boomers who worked for pensions and POCs dependent on handouts.

The dumb ingrates storm our land demanding our treasures and deference so stand up, man.

CONSERVATIVES ARE THE ONLY RELIEF

Brute strangers rob us blind, destroy our social fabric then demand we accept their predations.

80% of the women crossing the border get raped but when Trump called em rapists fems hate it.

Criminals are scared and desperate cuz they know the mean, stinking reality of globalism is evident.

The foes are like Bill Clinton: Ran as populist but governed as globalist. Be watchmen or be pist.

You ought to be careful with your society for in a minute it could be swept away from thee.

91% of Somali immigrants use welfare.   81% of Hispanics want bigger government.

COMMIES

No wonder leftist politicians applaud whites becoming a minority in their own country.

GLOBALISLAM: WHY WE DON'T WANT EM

Ladies and gentlemen: America has woken from her coma and we are rising!

A private unelected world body whose worldview & system is to dumb us down or exterminate us.

Globalism is such an unhappy thing: telling Africans they can't have ACs or we gotta stay poor: it stinks.

Globalist liberal pawns who know nothing hating Trump--yet every day the stock market are up!

Liberals want foreign secret TPPs running every facet of lives or foreign boards determining all things.

We see it everywhere: people don't wanna be lorded over by a big private corporate new world order.

The filthy globalists knew from their research that demoralized cultures are easily controllable.

The elites are perverts themselves, for evil is natural where God is absent.
It is more natural for man to sin than to repent.

Unelected, offshore, tax exempt with full immunity. And these guys rule over us with impunity?

The founders were afraid of this globalist threat but we'd need to stay moral, that's what they said.

Illegal immigrants blocking streets and protesting in a country not their own? Preposterous, deport em.

YOU LIBS DON'T CARE ABOUT US

You go against the American populist Donald Trump and that's the end of ya.

COMMIES

What are you doing in Los Angeles? All coasts are gone with Nemesis flyby. Go to center, stay alive.

Globalists wanna debase us--how better to do it but thru screeching music scaring dogs and cats?

They have it on everywhere--can't escape it: in stores, banks, restaurants-- this music is so inferior.

The whole world's under tyranny. Only a few have liberty without fear of government treachery.

The whole world wants to come here because we're free. So when they trash the founders, flee.

A constitution hems in governments (which tend towards tyranny) by protecting the individual.

Megyn said she hated Trump, was against guns, was an elitist/globalist and America said bye bye!

We bought into all the self-loathing and guilt. We took the blame for everything like it didn't quit.

The liberals like Eminem want no flag, no borders just welfare, terrorism and a new world order.

When left wing politics becomes a substitute for religion, that's all you have as you enter oblivion.

ALIENATION AND INSANITY

If the cost of sanity in society is alienation, I'll want solitude and freedom from those hating the nation.

Democrats spent 12 million to make up the story that Trump got urinated on in a hotel room.

Globalism is a new form of corporate colonialism, playing the nation states off against each other.

COMMIES

The anti-Trumpers are globalists selling their own country out. They've gotta hate it, or couldn't.

Globalists want to be rulers of the world (off our backs) so they hate Trump who's not out to get us.

With each day they don't get Trump out of office our victory accelerates. God showed up/changed fate.

Democrats are so evidently corrupt but the liberal deep state is so entrenched esp. on the bench.

Communist crap is boring but dangerous. Ignore their silly rants but stay prepared, they could injure us.

Everything you are seeing are desperation acts to cover up the crimes they have already committed.

What a time to be living, witnessing incredible unfolding: desperate acts most corrupt in history.

It's cool to hate white men. So when you hear it confront it cuz liberals are not your friends.

MENTALLY WEAK LEFTIST MEN

Leftist men weak mentally, six times more likely to steal. They pull down the strong/it's how they feel.

They got power over us by demasculinizing us, a nation of wimps cuz it's weak who love commies.

Trained to be fearful and broken down they're easily inducted into communism.

They could never defend values or even you or their own family: wimps, cogs in the wheel, a tragedy.

Communist bumper stickers indicate devil worship inside.

The weak pulls down the strong by the latter being convinced to let em run everything.

COMMIES

Made weak, they're told communism will make em strong if they overthrow the establishment.

Globalism is a satanic death cult/leftists are idiots wanting us in camps but they'll be first taken.

Marxism is going mainstream--we must fight this serious tragedy for people are getting mean.

Communists want a violent revolution--that's the hallmark of all they do-- expected in a day or two.

Millennial's HIGH acceptance rates of mass murder-enabling ideologies like socialism/communism.

The weak think they'll get a piece of the pie but they'll be the first to be killed cuz traitors: bye-bye

Creepy little nobodies always dream of the power they'll have in this big juicy bloodletting.

MORE FROM SOPHISTICATES: MATH IS RACIST?

"Math is racist" as the universities are creating fruit-loop craziness.

"Shakespeare is racist because he lived in a time of colonialism"--that's the kinda thing.

The idea that expanding is a white thing--as universities literally give degrees in mental illness.

Megyn Kelley went from teleprompter reading info babe to uncloaked globalist wanna-be bootlicker.

The globalists wanna cut your legs off with political correctness then give you a crutch.

They can make 10 X the money by NOT working in Germany than by working in the middle east.

COMMIES

We were a safe cocoon, a bubble of freedom in a sea of sharks and mayhem.

The unabashed drives to conquer, invade, impregnate were constrained.

World is a predatory, conflict-ridden, dangerous place of tribal warfare and thirst for domination.

The more you shield yourself from reality (by refusing to fear) the more you invite thieves and killers.

Hard times build strong men building good times breeding weak men building hard times.

Put all your stuff on the front lawn with a sign you've left for a month. It's the same when un-tough.

Envy showed cold steely silence as I showed him the house and his arms were folded in defiance.

I'm not putting up with it. It's of the devil, I have a fear of disorder and that's the end of it.

Trump's a germaphobe, I'm a disorderphobe and that's cuz heaven is orderly and Hell is a dirty mob.

You're a dam hick cuza how you live not how you were born.
Hell is dirty disorder, heaven is clean order so what's it gonna be poser.

There are no smart hicks just would-be geniuses.

COMPLACENT LASCIVIOUSNESS

The complacency of lazy lascivious liberals avoiding issues will get us into trouble about to ensue.

Relax, God can change variables and time. Take a break, resume sublime.

We gotta have a vaca--we've suffered so much, remember Obama?

Anyone who still loves and misses Obama is mentally ill or the worst traitor, so reject this poser.

COMMIES

These thugs and creeps like Eminem/Snoop are globalist sellouts dumbed by liberal dogma.

The promotion of sin is the elite's plan to debase the west so they can take down the best.

These devils make meticulous, ruthless, sadistic and indomitable plans out of jealousy of man.

Arabian nights was about excitement and adventure but no more cuz that tyranny has no allure.

Pope sold out to globalism. He thinks we're so dumb we'd buy climate change/invasions of barbarism.

There's so much debauchery we can take. Then they flip to the other side: Islam, a mistake.

Not "illegal aliens?" How about "foreign citizens criminally trespassing".

The Mexican gov conspires with illegals to get goods/services they don't wanna pay for--it's invasion at it's core.

We can't restore our civilization with someone else's babies. David knight

Chinese are funding anti-American films and buying Hollywood up while having babies here--must stop!

HOLLYWOOD SCUM TRAITORS

Hollywood: traitorous, evil and turned over to hatred of America where they have freedom--captured or dumb?

Chinese who have killed a billion of their own people are buying up Hollywood--could it get more evil?

There's a global re-alignment against world government as nationalism is exploding--elites panicking.

COMMIES

Enemy is squirming, scared and they don't know what to do. They're pulling all the stops but with out a clue.

Trump is the wrecking ball against the tyrannical planetary regime. The pyramid is in deep trouble I think.

We don't believe known liars CNN, we do our own research. Give up on them, even Fox is an obvious smirch.

Trump's support is expanding as he delivers his agenda. But the scum media says he's hated in America?

Accusing us of doing what they're doing. not news but a propaganda machine: disgraceful and boring.

When historically informed it's very frustrating as everything is in reverse and for some it ends in divorce.

Fake news says "it's terrible--he's obsessed on doing what he said he'd do"-- they're crazy/delusional too.

China producing movies as Trump a dictator to be overthrown--greater sedition than we've ever known.

The communist Chinese took over Hollywood illegally and traitor Obama allowed it to happen: let it sink in.

Trump has been waiting his entire life for this. Risen up, prepared and ready to catapult America up to bliss.

TRUMP IS PIGHEADED AND GREAT FOR IT!

Trump is so pigheaded it's beautiful. Not gonna compromise with lib professors, crazy women/juveniles.

Trump only loses if he doesn't deliver. But he's already done that a hundred times over: American caregiver.

Putin's trying to reconfigure world alliances due to our absence on the world stage under Obama.

COMMIES

The barbarians have entered the land, setting up idols to their sexual gods--as we face God's rod.

Trump'll use Mexico's anti-American hate to make him more popular, but first he gave you a chance, you gobbler.

Trump: You're gonna negotiate and make a deal that's good for everybody, or be run over--our guy's so clever!

Make a deal, or kneel. And he's got control of the greatest country to do it-- so proud of his greatness and appeal!

Chinese are bragging they're taking us over and though busy Trump's not doing enough on this, a no-brainer.

Will pay for the wall with 20% tax on Mexican imports. wow

Anti-Trumpers are making fools of themselves. Better jump ship you creeps or you'll soon be overwhelmed.

Uber smart Trump is the rare mix of genius intelligence, will and wit. The big magic elf, as great as it gets.

Gaslighting: When someone punches you in the nose and says they didn't do it. Like Obama lies, we outgrew it.

Hillary is in deep doo-doo. Trump's been nice, biding his time and getting the people in place for this coup.

Nasty signs and obscene chants giving your entire sex a bad name just cuz you can't find love and romance.

WITCHES ALWAYS PUTTING DOWN OUR MEN!

Always putting down our men! But not a word about rape culture of Islam-- feminists are even aligning with them.

Donald Trump is a man of his word. He told us what he's gonna do and now he's doing it--a new thing in our world.

COMMIES

He's over-delivering and I'm blown away, in the face of a negative onslaught of fake news of our day.

Nationalism's exploding everywhere especially with the linkup with UK--a new axis vs. evil globalism: Hurray!

Our guy can't be bullied. Not unsullied he's still doing good deeds and planting gold seeds: we are freed.

Evil loves evil and that explains these unholy alliances between strange groups of misguided people.

They jumped on the bandwagon to hate Trump cuz the establishment hates him--mere pawns, yuk.

Fake philosophers are hard-hearted. The progressives kill to rebuild so from the stiff-necked be departed.

Our constitution prevents harmful ideologies from eroding our values of freedom and equality.

Your kids are taught to be global citizens in a collectivist, sexually reckless, "sustainable" world.

The biggest lie of multiculturalism is: all cultures are alike. How stupid--some are lethal, e.g. 3rd Reich.

Unlimited tolerance leads to the disappearance of the truly tolerant and all tolerance with them.

"INCLUSIVE": THE MOST DANGEROUS WORD

The most dangerous word in our language today: "inclusive"--for some cultures are abusive.

We are taught to tolerate cruel things by "multiculturalism" or feared labels like "racism".

Relativism says "it's all good"--what baloney. There's a hierarchy in humanity and it's called liberty.

COMMIES

All cultures are not alike despite what relativists say. They are calibrated based on their humanity--okay?

Kim Jong Un, a madman who doesn't mind starving/killing his people, will be tested like never before. Potus

Socialist-Communist-Islamist. That's what we're becoming--are your family/friends enthusiasts?

Multiculturalism is the result of radical secularization: the mosques are built on the ruins of churches.

Progressive education teaches kids to love socialism. They have no idea what it really means, amen?

Sick socialists in Hollywood with hearts of wood: What traitors they are though freedom made them a star.

Gotta start judging those who won't judge barbarism! Don't let it pass--they're the worst humans.

Say to your liberal friends: "so, you condone barbarism?" Stress this point first, amen?

For dogs and cats things won't be getting better since the globalists see humaneness as a fetter.

Agree with globalism, the lowest common denominator? Eating horses, cats, dogs--to decency it's a mind-raper.

ILLEGAL IMMIGRATION CAUSES BLACK UNEMPLOYMENT

Illegal immigration: the main cause of black unemployment. Blacks: Trump's biggest supporters, amen.

Why is socialism always combined with race hatred? Because divide and conquer is their method.

If it's a democrat it's either a criminal or a commie. The former is justified and the latter is trendy.

COMMIES

Communism (socialism) is the scariest life on earth. You never know if they'll come for you first.

Don't succumb to arguing with their tendency to justify barbarity. It's you with the heart, a rarity.

Our sick mal-adaptation to mass immigration is to let 'em pee in the streets as our end is hastened.

People are becoming bloodthirsty (from the evil influence of ISIS) while the repentant think of eternity.

The barbarians are more like animals. And you wanna be nice to them? That is just not natural.

You let corruption and evil take over and you'll be brought low--destroyed--so keep em out: avoid.

This isn't immigration, it's invasion. Leftist leaders are invading their own countries and it's treason.

Americans aren't use to the raw side of reality--spoiled by two centuries of freedom and decency.

How to become fluent in any language: see it's the globalists. After a while this is so obvious.

Keep your mind focused on global elites and don't get distracted because it's all connected.

CHRISTIAN LEADERS VS. WORLD ORDERS

Putin and Trump have joined forces to defeat the New World Order, the major offender.

Socialism is leveling everyone so we're all equally poor. Then there's fascism at the top creating war.

Globalist "music" is "non-offensive" but it's boring, nonsensical, contrived and tasteless nonetheless.

COMMIES

The very people Bernie bashed were for socialism! The reason is: they're exempt from this system.

Why does socialism always lead to communism? It craves more in the rot of redistribution.

They act like it's the children's fault they're being raped by Muslims--told "don't provoke them".

It's not a religion but a conquering political system and it's not compatible with values of Christians.

The problem isn't radical Islam, it is ISLAM and the koran that looks down on women.

Inviting a sworn enemy into one's house is beyond stupidity, only of the devil--careful!

The media is jumping on Trump. Don't you see they're globalist lackeys--don't listen to this crud!

If Hillary or Bernie got in they'd have shut us all down. Tyranny always eliminates the profound.

All candidates even Obama said they were Christians. Look at what they do not what they say, amen?

"STANDS UP FOR WOMEN" BUT NOT CONSTITUTION

Hillary "stands up for women" but not the constitution? This is divide and conquer going into communism.

Pro-Americans expose the Marxist agenda of the UN global oligarchs and Hussein Obama: YUK.

When they say they're Christians don't listen because we don't need any more terrible lessons.

Mohammed told men to marry young girls for sex pleasure. Compare that to decency, our treasure.

COMMIES

You think it's okay to chop off heads, stone women and throw gays off buildings? You have no feelings.

Since it's not happening here, we're okay with it--but foes who wanna kill us can get here in a minute!

We see many works against a Christian to excite doubt and generate contempt and derision.

Voting for socialism is a form of immorality. That you think they should steal my stuff is insanity.

The more they come in the more they go with their religious convictions to rape us into Islam.

It's a planned invasion to destroy Christiandom. These are the young men of Islam.

Where we don't defend our faith--go on offense--we automatically lose it (lose all our defense).

Migrants to military bases while taxpayers fund mosques and Korans. Though we're Christians, that's the plan.

The more Islam, the less freedom--yet crazy liberals love them! Ban them I say, or total bedlam.

The extreme left bonds with Islamists because they too hate the west though it is the best.

Unaware that he was a rapist or that he tortured people of the day, Islam's just "different from Christianity".

NOT A RELIGION OF PEACE

It's not a tiny minority and it's not a religion of peace. They don't even object to terrorism, please!

Islam bonded with Nazis in WWII--why? Because the Nazis were tyrants and they hated Jews too.

COMMIES

Muslims standing against hate are targeted by the left, calling them "anti-Muslim bigots"--no jest.

Feminists and Islamists are aligned because they both hate free speech. Get that straight, I beseech.

Population Jihad is overtaking and flooding each and every one of us with masses until we're dead.

No one wants to be told their religion is wrong but wake-up: these are the lowest things in any throng.

The Krazy Kollege Kids actually want socialism. There is a dying need for Civics and true education.

Everyone's a dark liberal. It's the default setting, a warped worldview even seen in churchists too.

Liberalism is weird virtue signaling and it's embarrassing cuz they don't realize they're destroying.

They actually think they're good thinking these things. Globalist pawns as bankers pull the strings.

They're so arrogant about it then get angry on top of it like you're a mean cruel viper from the pits.

It happens especially in Germany with all their Nazi guilt only assuaged by flooding it with the antithetical.

FALLING AWAY: CHURCHES BECOME THE WORST

In fact the churches are becoming the worst, steeped in virtue signaling while facilitating invasion.

It's disgusting that churches don't see the value of patriotism: us first but we are relegated/cursed.

They've pushed the lie that patriotism is of the devil and only globalism (let em all in) is spiritual.

COMMIES

A false Christian's refusal to discipline creates criminals but then again one fears likely reprisals.

Why is someone from a foreign country more important than someone already here? Tell me, dear.

Having foreigners imposed on us like a flood--that's good? It's mean and you have hearts of wood.

Do you want a billion new people here? That's what no-borders means and stupidity should be feared.

To invade a culture (thinking it's a good thing) is so liberal: Impose, break in your door, throw a party.

Liberals wanna suck off of government, they love government--from the 60's, it's just the opposite.

Who'd wanna go on The View to argue with liberal shrews?

Stop worrying about stepping on toes. They've made us that way on purpose so show em you know!

It's psych warfare: They know how to stop speech, stop think, put you over the brink/make you drink.

They are so maudlin in their virtue signaling and "being nice". But then they quickly switch, yikes.

Trump represents the American ideal and loves this country. Left hates it, deplorables are a blessing.

AMERICA'S GREAT PROSPERITY IS TREACHERY?

Incomes are up, the highest ever: the Trump Effect is in effect cuz he's shrewd, brilliant and clever.

Tolerance marked Rome before the fall. We're jelly fish in it's grips as our wonderful country eats crow.

COMMIES

Globalism is not about ethnic food and world music. It's about tyranny that is utterly tragic.

Globalism: destroy nation state to bring in planetary government. Global elite occultists hate Christians.

How do we know Trump's the real deal? Cuz he's going after globalists--he knows how they steal.

Trump is seen as the buffoon among sophisticates but all of Europe agrees with him: keep em out.

Media concentrates on Trump the man rather than his policies on which America and Europe agrees.

They used "the children" as a trojan horse to bust our borders and destroy our sovereignty. Michael Savage

Boxer, Feinstein et. al. assert high heels over your head by catering to voting immigrants instead.

Muslim prayer rugs found on border. Was that one of the children? No it's our demise and disorder.

Open borders makes him a better Christian than us wanting America's sovereignty protected?

2139 DACA recipients convicted of crimes against Americans. But wait, they're just the children!

INVASION BY *MILLIONS* OF FIGHTING AGE MEN

Not children, they were grown men (many with gang tattoos) pouring over the border under Obama.

We're white and we exist too. We have a rich history and established the west yet hated as uncool.

So many rapes in Sweden they're not even investigating anymore. Just let em do it and lose the war.

COMMIES

Letting illegals vote devalues citizenship and shows contempt for the rule of law.

Our universities have abandoned all reason to be politically correct--can you imagine that?

Willfully and eagerly sacrificing everything on the altar of "diversity" and "inclusion": this is confusion.

All logic is gone, now everything's by rote: Stuff they've contrived while they boast.

Whenever liberals are in control illogic rules and they think it's cool as we're dictated to by fools.

The most profound truth of this generation: God is separate from His creation.

Oneism is an all-inclusive self-justifying cosmology: "personal empowerment" and "human flourishing".

Oneism understood: any notion of sexual morality must go, all sex is good.

The wise are intimidated by all-is-one politically correct thinking but the church is degrading.

UNIVERSITIES HAVE NO FREEDOM OF SPEECH

University says: Ideas should not be debated but repressed and the True Self never expressed.

With liberals in control it's an upside-down universe. Cronies aren't punished while we are cursed.

With liberals in control we put up with so much crap. Every day it's a new shoe to drop, a new map.

We are non-suicidal, non-nihilist, common sense constitutionalists.

Why did they distress us? Because they were liberals of course.

COMMIES

Feminism made men the adversary--but protection from a good man is your only hope missy.

How to get through the latter days: Do your own thing--what you're born for--before it's too late.

Dogs sense weakness and people do too. How people act before you get strong is what pushes you.

The most intelligent are really bashed in this generation as the dumbed are compelled to aberration.

The crazy Hillary/Pelosis are on fruitcake level power trips. So arrogant, mentally ill and fallen: ick!

With this kind of weakness, evil blindness and deadly ignorance the whole world is laughing at us.

I pray the old American spirit explodes as we fight the animating contest of liberty from toads.

They want to see their own president as a failure--how pathetic they are!

California's soft-on-crime mentality made us a victim and it's the same in all liberal cities and towns.

ANTI-ESTABLISHMENT BECAME ESTABLISHMENT

The anti-establishment become the pro-establishment having enjoyed the trappings of office.

When we saw massive liberal bureaucracies fail those in the know got outa the California hell.

If you're watching movies all day you're a dry well to the household, all contributions gone.

What are you contributing, you bore? Sucked into a vortex of media but nothing coming out anymore.

COMMIES

No man would ever sit thru a woman's meeting: so boring in fact, an hour I'll never get back.

You waste your own time so wanna waste mine.

They say they're "fashionably late" when it's just their ego that loves to make em all wait.

Don't call it "hanging with God's people" when it's just chattering like all the silly sheeple.

The virtue signaling going on in women's gatherings is very boring but it's all about identity.

ONLY VIRTUOUS WOMEN CAN RULE

In women's meetings there's usually one doing the talking while the others are listening intently.

These aren't days of Roy Rogers. We got creeps coming to Cane Beds just like all neighborhoods.

How interesting: the far right is actually the new centrism marking a return to historical realism.

As Trudeau's progressivism is dying and depleting Canadian conservatism is exploding and Christian.

Secular liberalism has no room for white men having painted itself to the corner of identity politics.

VINDICTION AGAINST NEIGHBORS

Trump: Call the cops with tip that the neighbor's crazy so they go get the guns and arrest him: scary!

Do we adapt to the left's superstitious hysteria or revert to reason and logic in our America?

They've invested so much into this they can't deal with the terrible unforeseen consequences.

COMMIES

You're gonna punish me cuz a lunatic shot up schools? So with home invasion, I can't shoot?

It's so disgusting. Men having fun with their butt buddies telling their wives they've gone fishing.

He always says it's a small thing but it's no small thing it hurts her so deeply she's sick and trembling.

The lady said "I'm very scared of it happening again--another way of saying I just don't trust him."

Survivor's clue: It will never be over and you don't know the half of it.

We all know that people can't get well for other people if they don't even see themselves as sick/evil.

What's to stop him from doing it again? His love for you? That didn't work five times re: sin.

Lesson: It's not that he did it it's that he would do it, he's into it.

The lady said "he hurt me so much I can't breathe and naturally he minimizes it." I hear this.

Women vote like their husbands cuz that's why they married (affinity) not cuz he's making them.

What about husbands voting as their wives say, Hillary? That's more likely to be the case, silly.

Why are big corporations allowing radical leftists into company decisions regarding language?

THE PC MARCH OF STUPIDITY

The politically correct march is like a contest of stupidity as our jaw drops with each new absurdity.

COMMIES

Interlocking jealousy triangles: if I pet those dogs my own dogs might react with fear and anger.

Christian men must learn the importance of not hurting their wives by what they see with their eyes.

Obama shipped guns into Mexico to blame the second amendment and kill those who object.

Taking all our identities: Trudeau the worst globalist banned the word "mother" just today.

Banning "mother" and "father" is not tolerance but taking our identities and a cultural slaughter.

Banning word "mother" (may make someone feel bad) is not tolerance but an identity-crusher.

If you want smaller government, white males and white married females is your demographic.

You cross that line (of debauchery of swine) then you're on the treadmill to hell without shame/guilt.

LIBERALS CAN'T ACCEPT DEFEAT

Libs continue to pound that Hillary won, as if our founders ever wanted rule by a mob.

We elected someone to clean it up and he's doing it—looking up!

Fascism came to America under the guise of liberalism: total control/no freedom.

After Hillary Clinton, Maxine Waters and many other feminists people might disdain having women in office.

They don't care about Benghazi, Kidafi, Haiti or Pizzagate (etc. etc. etc.) they just love Hillary.

Virtue signaling/identity politics: a fraud but women suck it up to be mod.

COMMIES

Here's the same old divide, women. Only one solution, don't talk to em.

Unable to see their faults they assume it's prejudice against women. Their own denial blinds them, again.

There is right and wrong. Absolute morality, not relativism of the throng.

That's not killing it's defending against an aggressor coming against you or it's an unjust war/sinning.

It's so scary how much women love Hillary not caring what she's done whether Kadafi, Haiti or Benghazi.

Hillary could get in if enough dumb women or wimpy feminist men.

Weak leaders have paralysis in fear of retaliation.

If the church doesn't talk of sin they're just social hall religion, a need to be seen and so incredibly boring!

CHURCH OMITS SIN—THE MAIN THING

All wars began with a false flag to gin up support. WWII killed 50 million and the left wants nuclear--come Lord!

A Christian holiday. How wholesome, how sweet, a rare treat, a meaningful revival to ruminate about and tweet.

Truth is the opposite to appearances, based not on what everyone thinks (herd view) but on facts and sciences.

Juan and Geraldo are boring, liberal, aggravating speedbumps yet they're on FOX constantly. Yuk.

Why would Assad wanna kill his own people? He's a crazy man in a country filled with factions, many evil.

Conservative = textualist, by the book.

COMMIES

No analysis of Hillary allowed: Benghazi, emails, Libya were just pseudo-scandals, stuff made up, fowl.

Why they cry? Because their savior, light itself, Athena was extinguished: archetype, demolished.

If they assimilate it's different but if they don't they're "citizens", right? Liberals don't care about our life.

After getting news focus on inner peace or die--for "men's hearts will fail them" from fear or media lies.

I wouldn't go down that path lest you be cast in that light as a shrew. It's sickening, blue, dirty too.

So you have the money to make a complete fool of yourself, in public no less.

Can't do your destiny if always thinking about the past. You're not getting any younger/have a blast.

Your generation's nuts so stop reflecting the ASS and think for your own self so later no remorse.

Experiments on dogs and monkeys--the SJW's don't care about that, they just scream as always.

Do anything you want, you're never get our guns cuz that leaves us defenseless against thugs.

Insanity in Fashion without Logic or Function: That's what you see on runways of America and Europeans.

Old age is like Joe Biden: Sometimes your up/sometimes down but the downs are happening more often.

WOMEN OF THE HOUSE

Yes it's true, women [for survival] plan ahead and get things setup for the new life not here yet.

What else can we do? Being alone is suicidal, we must get things set up and it's smart to do so.

P.S.

Liberal family members are always offended. That's their whole thing when coming against the splendid.

They create false narratives--to protect you from--but you don't know it as they dumb you down.

What to tell your scared kids: the left did this, demonizing Mr. Trump and making him monstrous.

The left is ALWAYS irate over it's own false narrative.

THE HERD IN WORDS
HIX POLITIX
HOW THEY RUINED US
JUST SKIP DINNER
LE FEMME AND THE COMMUNIST SPIRIT
LIBERAL CHAOS & ROT
LIBERAL DOUBLETHINK
LIBERAL GALL 1 & 2
LIBERAL SHOVE-DOWNS
LOCK YOUR GATE
LOSERS and Femme Fatales
MANUAL FOR SUPERIOR MEN
MODERN ART FROM HELL
MOSTLY FAKE
NOTES TO CHAMPS 1 & 2
OVERCOME FRENEMIES
PC MAKES US CRAZY
PEOPLE ARE CRUEL
PEOPLE PROBLEMS 1 & 2
PERSECUTED GENIUIS
POLI-PSYCH MYSTERIES
PRETENTIOUS SLOBS
QUEEN BEE
RED NEW DEAL
RETURNING TO FIRST NATURE
SEASON OF TREASON
SEPARATE MEANS HOLY
SOCIAL HYPNOTISM
SOLITUDE SOLUTION
SUPERCILIOUS
THE SCHOOLS SCREWED EM UP
TOAD TO PRINCE
TRIALS CYCLES
TRUMP VS. GROUP
TRUST IN TRASH
THE TRUTH ABOUT PEOPLE
UNDERHEANDEDLY CLEVER
WALK TALL WITHIN WALLS
WE'RE NOT ALL ONE
WINNERS SKIP DINNER
WORK OR SMERK

100 KAREN KELLOCK BOOKS

AFFINITY OR MISERY
AGELESS CORNUCOPIA
AMERICA AWAKE!
AMERICA'S DAFT ERA
ARTS OF PALEO FASTING
AUTOPHAGY ON CHEATERS
BACKSTABBING NEUROTICS
BETRAYAL TRAUMA
BOOMERS AND BROKENNESS
BOOT ON NECK
CHAMPION GUIDES
COMMIE NUTHOUSE
COMMIES
COMMUNIST SPIRIT
CONTAGION OF MADNESS
CONTAGIOUS MADNESS
CULTURE CLASH BASHED
DAFT LEFT
DAILY FASTARIAN
DAM RATS
DIVERSITY IS CRUELTY
E-RACE WHITE
EVIL FREAKS (Beyond Gross)
THE END OR A BEND?
FEMALE BULLIES AND FEMI-NAZIS
FEMALE CARNALITY
FEMALE DUMB DOWN
FEMALE POWER DRIVE
FEMINISM AND RUIN 1 & 2
FIX FOR MISFITS
FOOLS & TRAMPS
FREEDOM SPEAKING
FRENEMY ENABLER
FRENEMY LIAR
FRENEMY THIEF
FRENEMY TRAITOR
TRENEMY TYRANT
GENIUS IS HELD DOWN
GLOBALISLAM
GOD USES THE FLAWED
HAZE OF THE LATTER DAYS

KAREN KELLOCK PH.D.

M.S. Political Science, San Diego State. Ph.D. in Psychology, University of California Irvine. Postdoctoral: UCI School of Medicine, Dept. of Psychiatry [NIMH Grants]. Developed the Debris Theory of Disease, a theory of system pathology in 120 books and 22 textbooks for the general public. The theory has a general formula: All disease is obstruction, all recovery is elimination, all success is attraction. The three obstructions are people, habit and food. Remove obstruction and snap to your goals, waiting in the wings.

www.ingramcontent.com/pod-product-compliance
Lightning Source LLC
Chambersburg PA
CBHW061729250726
48657CB00002B/838